The Other Woman

I warned you

Serena J.

Self -Published Autobiography

ISBN: 9798530260346

DEDICATION

To my beautiful mother - Faye Richmond

CONTENTS

ACKNOWLEDGMENTS

I would like to thank all of those that helped me through,
and those that continue to stand with us.
God is a very present help; without Him we fail.

There is no better place than peace.

1 CREPT IN

He told me about her, so she was not a total stranger. I had seen her back in the day so her kind was easy to spot. I'm not the kind to name drop but you will see what I mean in a minute. She had relatives and friends; you know- BIRDS OF A FEATHER- sort of peeps. They had the same look in the eyes. Dressed nice but it was a disguise.

 I was well aware of her, and so we prayed together that she was a thing of the past.

I did not realize that she was a stronghold. I didn't see that she called him from time to time, and that he had answered and had to hang up on her. I didn't perceive that she would meet him at the front door every time he opened it and he would battle her in silence just to go to the store, I did not discern that it was a tug-of-war to not run off with her alone in a vacant parking lot, and just come back and tell me the reason it took him so long was because he couldn't find what I sent him after...

She would scratch his itch; an itch that I had prayed to God about, that I yelled and screamed that I held him by the tail of his shirt about, but nothing would help, he would run to the other woman.

She came knocking when I was gone when I wasn't tending to my home when he was feeling all alone.

I lost him 6 months in- just six months with a vicious blow (lost a job-that he thought would define him again, but he had to stand and see that he remained still).

She would eventually win him over. He would spend most of his time with her on the back deck, he would enjoy cooking and she would be in the kitchen with him. He would get some fresh air; she always accompanied him.

He would stay up late- I would always be a crowd so my presence would mean their absence. If we were watching a movie together, he would go wash dishes or fold clothes and take them upstairs, doing just anything sometimes to get to her. I eventually just stayed upstairs in the bedroom and he stayed downstairs... I found no need to be where I wasn't wanted. He never said it but it just was such a hide a seek game that I couldn't stand the games anymore. Some days I couldn't take it, so I would EXPLODE! Some days she would get him to explode on me and he would be so mad because I wouldn't say a thing just minding my business because my peace disturbed their chaos.

If he had been off that day when I would come home after work it would be apparent that he had been with her. My drive home was one of prayer of what I would face.

 It was obvious he had been intimate with the other woman for a period of time that day because her scent was left all on him and in my home. It would break me when I would confront him about it; he would become defensive of her and lash out if he could for the shame.

I had had all I could take; one of us had to go. It had come time for me to see who he wanted. He said I could leave. So basically, he said that she was moving completely in! The other woman would no longer be crept around the corner and in other rooms, but just within arm's reach. He chose her over me. She had a mean reach on him.

Who was this man? My baby would never say such things to me like that. She had her claws in him, she had changed him! He was putting me out, allowing me to leave.

2 BETTER OR WORSE

I am tired, it's now a struggle to stay. I have to relinquish my marriage because the fight has been fought. I swung and I stood my ground and was disrespected; I prayed and cried I laid hands in the name of Jesus, we cried together- I screamed and even left home but nothing worked!

The other woman always came back worse and winking. Someway somehow, she had a way with him that I didn't; she could comfort him in ways that I couldn't and my he had a love for her.

I couldn't watch it any longer. He would go on outings with her and the time I would ask for the money it would be gone.

Most times I would try to get the bill money on payday but per chance I couldn't, that is what would occur.

He said he should be able to just do what he wants in his own home- with the other woman. Lord I know you are not slack of your promises, what is the way you are taking me?

The grip grew tighter, he sunk deeper into her snares that grind him to shreds. He appeared all the more ashamed and disgusted, but all the more continued because he didn't know how to tell her to go.

He rushed me away so that he could hurry and run to be with her, to pick her up. I ran into him once on the way home after service one Sunday, and he had detoured towards one of her many homes. He couldn't wait to

leave the house of the Lord for this;
My heart was broken...

I rooted for him, I cheered for him, I prayed for him. I saw the cycle continue and worsen at times. I made it through with the help of the Lord; the other woman still remained.

 I wanted the man I married, and the truth of the matter was- this was the man I married. I married the masked him. (frowning emoji).

He never left a lot of things of his past, he never left and cleaved. He still gripped so tightly to his childhood and was there mentally and it's hard when you won't let go and be healed.

 It's a hard way when you won't let go. I knew this for myself, I dealt with it too.

I tried to be silent about things, but the other woman just kept getting louder! So, I scream! I push all the buttons that have pushed mine and that was a horrible thing.

 I went for broke in making sure I am heard and understood, but they are drunk off of each other's ego so my words do not stay because they cannot comprehend sound conversation. I was infuriated! I was in their world all alone and no one knew what I was going through. I was living a private hell. A marital violation an abuse.

3 HOME WRECKER

My home was not my beautiful place of refuge, my well-kept home; it's a constant mess because of the other woman. She is filthy, and she slings food and trash and clothes everywhere. She is unorthodox, unstable, unclean, unholy, and unwanted! I still fight for us!!

He had begun to ignore my calls, so I was convinced that was by her persuasion. He is never available to me or for me. I call and the rejection rings on- my call was declined. So glad to know God hears us when we call Him, but at that moment, my God man was failing me. Both of us had misplaced my eyes.

The situation continues our Pastor knows; we have counseled with him, but to no avail. The prayers continued.

Due to the unrest I am advised to be safe which means at all cost. I am to get out of harm's way; physical, emotional, and spiritual.

The best thing I could hear was do not stay to be damaged any further. I thought, at this point I am the most damaged I could be. I know this because I try to hurt him due to the hurt, he has inflicted upon me.

He doesn't even believe the control she has over him it's demonic. The words that come out of his mouth are not even his own they are the other woman's.

So, when I do get those few moments alone with him, I recite what was said, either with the recording or with my words. He listens with disbelief. It's a sobering factor. He cannot believe that this is his voice that he is listening to.

Fussing and acting like a monster. But it is the other woman sitting on his lap who is actually doing all the actions speaking all the words. He apologized, shame rolls across his face, but that wasn't the objective!

Please don't go to her when you are in pain when I sit right in front of you. I am frightened of her reach.

He has run from the truth and literally ran into a wall with his truck-at this point!!

Scrapped the entire side so he thinks he is safe and the other woman just laughs as if this is all a game.

I thank God for sparing his life yet again.

He is so controlled by her I just don't know how to function with him anymore.

He is arrested by her and she has him bound. He is found behind bars and imprisoned due to his relationship with her. She drags him into a hole that others have to dig him out of but its only for her benefit. GOD HELP US- HELP HIM!

Free him from her chains! Help him see he is bound!

Stuck in the unknown of my brokenness: heart and home; I must face the reality of the insanity. Same routine, with no new results.

I move from the threat of leaving to giving a date and boxing are now being filled with items to signify

I mean business! I packed up the remains of our broken home in hopes of a mend. The other woman destroyed all the things I loved- items and my husband. Things I brought into this marriage that my children made me, she broke them.

She tore down my loving husband to be this twisted man that I could hardly recognize or trust.

I look for new homes, hoping he would miss me before I am gone and try to rebuild this one, but that other woman curls around him like a snake.

It's like at any given moment he loses his voice and to be free from her and she takes over.

I continue plans to leave hoping to stay but I knew I couldn't live in those conditions.

Too dangerous. I would let my landlord know of our final day in the townhouse. 25 more days now.

I just cannot bear to watch anymore of this self-destruction.

4 THE PART

I honestly will say that I do not want this to be our final end. I want this to end and to end now, but as you can see that is not up to me. I promised myself I would never come 2nd again. How frightening that this is my marriage!

I have faith in God and His healing power and ability to deliver. But it's my husband's faith that is being weighed too and we are in this together and I cannot fight alone and we cannot keep fighting in the manner that we had been.

I question whether this marriage was even desirable for him to want, or else she wouldn't have been his go-to.

He was distant to me and everyone, and just wanted to be alone and that's when I later found out that it was to spend so much time with her.

 Am I not enough? Yes, I am! Although he wants her, I know that the Lord loves me and is Jealous for me and always has arms open wide for me.

Lord I will need you to heal my broken heart.

She has taken a toll on him. I can tell he is tired of her, but he doesn't know how to quit her.

She has been a mainstay, a trusted-rusted, friend, a crutch, for so long, he acts like he can't make a move without her, (and I am the wife).

 I continue to pack and pray; his soul is in the balance.

He is getting lucid and downright transformed he is being overtaken by her. He is a puppet to her. The conversations are full of fury and rage. There is a hatred and cry for the hurt-hearted him.

I am so angry at her for bringing this up. She is an instigator a constant stickler. She is pride at the height of a twin tower that collides inside of him. She is his thorn in the flesh that causes his downfall. But he cannot see it.

Will, Our love live? After he had wined and dined her, and cooked with her, watched movies with her, spent quality time with her sometimes, not much, but sometimes, he felt guilty and remembered me and found his way to me.

I have tried for hours to get him to come to me but he wanted her intimacy first.

And because I knew that I would refuse him but he would always say you are my wife bringing in the obligation of the vows and, made me feel guilty because I was his wife as he said.

It's like being in a distasteful relationship without your consent or regard. It's enough to cause me to lose my appetite and it always turned my stomach.

It's a constant warzone. My mind is scrambled, did I mention that I feel like I am losing it? She tries to make me feel like I have failed him by taunting me when he isn't looking.

I can hardly sleep; fearful, anxious, still- watchful, prayerful. I rest knowing that if she wants to take me out of here, I did try for my husband when I did.

I would walk with him the rest of the way if he would just leave her alone. But the chemistry between them is obvious and unbearable.

I assure him that space between us is necessary, because this isn't working and we are miserable, well at least I am and I need to have peace, remain safe and feel secure when I am in my own home.

I am witnessing this love affair he has with this other woman right before my eyes and I am exhausted in every way. We have come to the wall of reasoning. Yes, he has sought counsel and treatment for his addiction to the other women but it was short lived. This now is a matter of life or death for us both.

5 BIG STEP

The call is made to our leadership (Pastor) and we are well advised that this is a healthy step towards healing. So, I proceed, because he doesn't see anything wrong.

I strategize when and where, but the urgency will cost me if I wait much longer. I began to pack up what's left of our home that didn't get destroyed. All of my movement triggered her to meanness as usual and agitation, so I tried to do most of the packing when they were not around. I talk about the separation only when she is nowhere in sight due to the irritability.

The other woman just thunders through everything and attempts to make my words lies and make belief.

Whispering to him that I am a psychopath; at this point my mood swings are aroused by what I witness.

Lord help me!!

 She is trying to drag me into their world of chaotic consumptions of each other. I don't want any parts! I will not accept this mental anguish any longer.

The boxes are packed and the date is set! They cannot stay according to the landlord. With that news for them they have to be pushed daily to prepare and pack, it's a joke to them. They sit and toy with each other instead.

I purchase a storage building. I reserve the U-Haul. I call to disconnect services within the home. This is really happening after two and a half years.

My heart is broken, but I have a strength I cannot explain. It's a strength that I want to sit in a corner and die but I cannot and I must see this through. I press on.

She sits on his lap on the couch where they fellowship the couch that broke the camel's back. This love affair honestly is not fair to us, we are being robbed with the doors wide open and a welcomed greeting. I let go and let God; I trust Him with my life.

The car is packed and my storage building is full. I leave my keys for the landlord. The remaining things he takes to store with him. I now am staying with family.

He is a good man! I don't understand what more can make this work; hopefully time.

I won't stop trying, although we are apart and his mind is made up for now.

Love has happened but it hasn't bloomed into the rosebush of charity I am positive it could be. Instead it is a thorny thicket.

The very thing I was afraid to have was given to me. It did what I have been protecting myself from.

I stand at the door ready to leave for the last time; he halfheartedly says let's talk about us but he knows there's no us with her on his hip and at his every beckon and call.

I pray for him to love me back soon, to choose me and not her and all I stand for. I am not perfect. I Pray for him to wake up.

But until then, I stand and look at my husband with his mistress, the one he loved most, and is full of her venom. I silently pray and ask God not to let that venom enter my heart and form a boulder of bitterness. Let me love again; allow me to be loved. Love me Jesus until that moment comes...

I exchange words of reasoning for the millionth time, and say good bye. I get inside my tightly packed car with the remaining things and head to my temporary place of residency with tears rolling down my face.

6 NEW CHAPTER

It is quite easy to just go on in life as if nothing is a big deal, when in fact... IT'S A VERY BIG DEAL!! Especially if you are like me.

I never knew that on that Monday night I would meet my husband, my love. I would later see him to be handsome and so sweet. A heart of gold I tell you.

Prior to my meeting him I must tell you what happened.

I had a longtime friend that I had lost contact with for many years to get in touch with me. He was a gentleman and never crossed any boundaries in my life and I meet him many years before I came back to The Lord.

My mind started wondering and I began to wonder is this a God connection...

We texted and we connected within fifteen minutes and had a wonderful conversation as always!! My heart was racing; I was protecting myself and felt safe at the same time. Lord let your will be done was my prayer.

I discovered later within conversations that our friendship was still just that. He wanted children and I was -clearly done with that, and he hadn't found the right women just yet to start a life and family with. My heart went out to him, and I told him jokingly to stop being so picky. He was such a good person and life was not going just how he had planned it at 40 though.

Weeks later, I remember sitting at my dining room table in my apartment one evening when it hit me... I just may be alone for the rest of my life!

I felt upset with myself for allowing myself to get excited that my friend could be the one because a slight part of me felt rejected again even though that wasn't even the case. After all, why would he try to locate me after all these years? Why was he going through the trouble to catch me up on his life and what he was going through? He couldn't be that stupid to not accept me as I am and come to know Jesus with me.

I mean what's wrong with me.

I was allowing the enemy to play me when all along it was a fog of compromise and conformity that was in front of me in the form of rejection!

I began to repent and cry out to the Lord for allowing myself to get in this predicament; I was sorrowful. Godly sorry (2 Corinthians 7:10)!

 I was upset yes; I was still alone correct, but I had the Lord! I began to tell God, with tears streaming down my face that I accepted His plan for my life! I no longer wanted to wonder this far in my mind thinking that the next man was my potential husband or mate...

I wanted whatever it was that God wanted me to have; even if it meant a life of singleness! No!

I was not putting my heart through my own rejection when I have not been.

Yes, I cried out and self-delivered that day and surrendered my secret heart's desire into the Lord's hands; I would no longer hide in the shadows of fig leaves of saying one thing and being another.

I would no longer have a Nicodemus mentality to hide above others in the darkness of hopeful interaction with those that walked on earth in the normality of following Christ in the direction he was going; how else will we know or see what miracles He will perform.

I surrender that day right on the spot-

I released my hurt; I released my will I

released my love to Christ. I wanted to dive into serving the Lord with my whole heart from that day forward.

I got in the press from that day, or so I thought. I decided to not let myself hurt myself again!

The Lord had called me, I know there is a call to prayer and a word somewhere inside of me; I know that he wants to reign in my life so all I needed to do was allow Him.

7 FOCUSED

I would prepare to let my friends and sisters in the Lord to know what my decision was. They always wanted to see me with someone or tell someone they knew about me, but I would just laugh it off and tell them no thank you. They loved me and just wanted what I secretly wanted for myself also.

Yes, I will come down from this place that I had been hiding. That no one else, unless discerned could see.

In that place I felt rejected when that wasn't even the case. I confessed that I'd never be there again.

The enemy wanted me to get all in my feelings in the name of the Lord.

I felt as if I had done so much in my past that I didn't deserve anyone. I would be the eunuch of the group.

I began to think about Hannah in 1 Samuel and how she was sorely vexed because she had not had a child yet- her womb was closed, she wasn't barren! Peninnah was having child after child, but her husband loved Hannah so much more than Peninnah the other wife. He gave her more because he loved her more. She was blinded by her longing for a child and never saw what was right before her. She wanted to bear a child. She had been delayed she had thought but she was not denied.

As women many times, we want just what our girlfriends have, and in this case just what our enemies have.

She had the love and care of a wonderful husband who didn't understand why he was never enough? Saying to her am I not more than ten sons? We are the same way when God blesses us, and we don't get that one thing we have been praying for.

 God blesses us way beyond what we deserve, but we can't see it for focusing on what we want, declaring and decreeing it!

The faith is wonderful, but we must not forget when we stand in faith, God grants us on His time, and we must trust the process. It's in His word like this:

Now faith is the substance of things hoped for, the evidence of things not seen. (Hebrews 11:1)

Keep on waiting and trusting; only believe!

So, there I was like Hannah, realizing I'm never going to see the side of life I secretly longed for. God will withhold nothing good from us. He knows just what we need. Timing is everything. It brought me to tears, just as she cried out so did I.

God had heard her heart before she had asked. God knew, and He never makes a mistake- we say that but when it comes to us, we are confused as to why our prayer wand didn't move our mountain of mistrust.

We think we can tell God when and how to handle our situation.

 The truth is this...

We pray and intercede for others.

 We go to God on behalf of someone else and we trust that God will move on their behalf and so we wait on the praise report and while we wait, we praise God for the outcome.

And then it comes to us, and our prayer needs that we take to God. We pray and ask Him, them if it doesn't happen what we can say in "adequate time," we go back to Him like He forgot.

8 INFORMATION

So, I was meeting with a few of my girlfriends for our weekly Olive Garden lunch date. We so enjoyed those times.

Anyway, as we were seated and our order was taken, conversations began. I began to share with them my decision.

 I advised them of what God could do better if I would just block out the thought of having a significant other. They were so understanding and supportive. We enjoyed each other's company, conversation, and great meal.

Now I am free from ever worrying indirectly about it!

Shew what a feeling I was off to a new start.

One day after work while scrolling through social media I received a message from a Pastor to come and attend and lead out in prayer at his Church. I messaged that I would contact my Pastor for his blessing and get back in touch with him.

 My Pastor consented and I contacted within that week that I would be there as requested.

On the day of prayer, I set out early to look for a car. It was a long process, and I made a few stops and applications but will look again another day. I had to get ready for prayer. I had prayed within all day.

I called a friend, and she loaned her car for me to get there, and my daughter and I headed towards Intercessory Prayer in Virginia about an hour away.

The weather was rough with April showers. Reporting storms for the evening, and the storms were bad lately; like tree ripping! I was hesitant to go with the weather report momentarily, but I felt the press of the Lord and went on. Trusting God to protect us and keep us all during the meeting at the church.

We arrived and the prayer began. I started intercessory prayer as the Pastor freed me to do so and the saints and I prayed, and we prayed through. I was on a cloud of glory basking in the presence of the Lord.

As we closed, I embraced the saints, and was embracing a sister when a gentleman came up and asked for a hug. No problem, I gave him a side hug and my daughter, and I walked towards the door to head to the parking lot.

It seemed that this gentleman followed us outside. No biggie we all were leaving but he followed us to the car. He then asked if I would be at our district meeting that would be coming soon and I said yes. He said he may be there, and we said goodbye to him and others.

I rode home on a heavenly cloud by the move of God in prayer that night.

9 CONNECTION

Maybe two days later, I received a message on social media from someone I didn't know. It was from the gentleman from the prayer meeting under another name.

 I was a bit indignant about his approach thinking he was hiding something, so I was very upfront with my questions. He explained somewhat and stated also that he thought that I would be a good person to talk to.

 I advised him that I wouldn't mind civil Godly conversation and I would advise him as far as I could by the leading of the Lord.

We began to message back and forth a few days a week and it eventually ended up that he requested to speak on the phone.

I was nervous about that but agreed. He was a very soft-spoken man; quiet, attentive and a great listener.

We had a connection from our incidences or coincidences and could relate to one another from these points. When he was telling me something that I knew was not going to work and not what I am going for, God at one point told me to listen to him and hear him out and so I listened!

I wonder if I willed him to be mine against all odds? Did I listen and not pray the will of God for both of our lives...?

To be continued... Sequel.

ABOUT THE AUTHOR

Serena J. is still separated from her
husband. Healing from the pain.
Becoming a friend. Finding herself.

It's a lesson or a blessing or both!

Contact@ serena2210@yahoo.com

Serena J.